Doing My Job

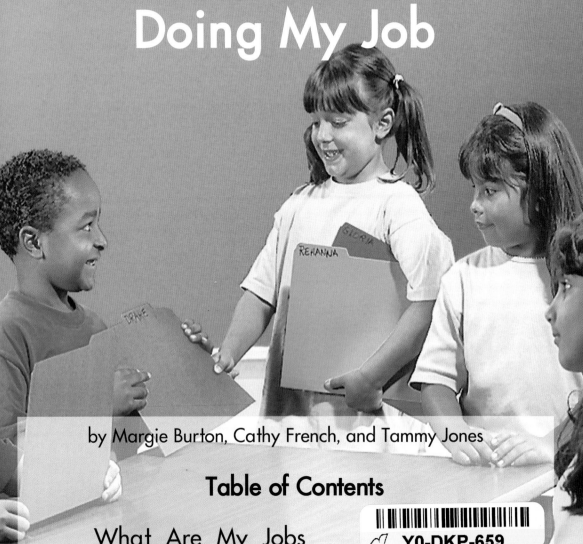

by Margie Burton, Cathy French, and Tammy Jones

Table of Contents

What Are My Jobs at Home?

I have jobs to do at home.
Here I am helping with the groceries.

I do a lot of jobs every day.

I have many jobs to do.
When I get up, I make my bed.

I help set the table for breakfast, too.

I put out the plates, cups, forks, and knives. I fold the napkins.

What Are My Jobs At School?

At school I have jobs to do, too.
It is my job to read to my teacher.
My teacher helps me do my job.

Sometimes it is my job to help my teacher.
I carry things for her.

I pass out
the folders, too.

What Are My Jobs After School?

I am on a soccer team after school. It is my job to help our team score.

It is my job to play fairly.

I try to pass the ball to my friend.
He is a good soccer player.
But it is my job to help him!

My friend scores points for our team in almost every game.

It is also my job to be a good sport, even when we do not win.

I sing with my friends.
It is my job to sing the best
that I can.

Another job I have is to smile when I sing. When people see all of us smiling, they know that we like to sing for them.

I have to do many jobs every day!

Doing jobs helps me become a more responsible person.